Practice for pupils who are New to English!

This fantastic CGP book is ideal for Primary pupils who are 'New to English' (English proficiency Band A).

New vocabulary is introduced in a clear, friendly way, with scaffolded activities so pupils can begin to form their own sentences.

And that's not all! We've also included free audio files so pupils can listen and repeat — you can find them at this page:

www.cgpbooks.co.uk/EAL-book-one

What CGP is all about

Our sole aim here at CGP is to produce the highest quality books — carefully written, immaculately presented and dangerously close to being funny.

Then we work our socks off to get them out to you — at the cheapest possible prices.

Contents

How to Use this Book 4

About Me 8
Making sentences to describe yourself and saying what you like doing.

Part 1

Section 1 — Nouns & Pronouns

Colours and School Equipment 10
Combining singular nouns with adjectives; 'a' becoming 'an'.

Numbers and Toys 12
Combining numbers 1-6 with singular and plural nouns.

Section 2 — Verbs

Transport 14
Writing sentences using 'There is' and 'There are'.

Healthy and Unhealthy Food 16
Saying 'I like' and 'I don't like'; using 'and' and 'but' to join clauses.

Talking about Pets 18
Making sentences and questions using 'can' and 'can't'.

Numbers and Parts of the Body 20
Combining numbers 1-12 with singular and plural nouns; using the verb 'to have'.

Section 3 — Adjectives & Prepositions

Talking about Feelings 22
Using adjectives of emotion after 'I'm'.

At the Beach 24
Making sentences and questions which include prepositions of place.

Section 4 — Maths Language

2D and 3D Shapes 26
Naming different shapes; describing the colour, size and properties of shapes.

Part 2
Part 2 revisits and builds on what has been learned in Part 1.

Section 5 — More Nouns & Pronouns

Describing Clothes 28
Using an apostrophe and 's' to show possession; using possessive adjectives.

Section 6 — Verbs & Word Order

Days of the Week 30
Using the verb 'to be' in the past, present and future tenses.

My Family 32
Using personal pronouns; making sentences that use third person present tense verbs.

The Weather 34
Using the verb 'to be' in the past, present and future tense; saying when things happen.

Wild Animals 36
Testing understanding of subject-verb word order.

Morning Routine 38
Making sentences using time connectives.

Things I Like to Do 40
Using regular and irregular verbs in the simple past.

Celebrations 42
Avoiding overuse of the past progressive.

At the Playground 44
Making sentences which include prepositions and adverbs.

Phonics

Letters and Sounds 46
Testing a range of phonemes and letter formation.

Phonics Progress Chart 47
Checking knowledge of letters and sounds.

Short Vowels 48
Checking children can tell the differences between short vowel sounds.

About the Authors

Sally Roberts is a KS2 EAL advisor, teacher trainer and Advanced Practitioner in EAL in the East Midlands. She has specialised in second language acquisition for nine years and has supported over 200 KS2 children through the early stages of learning English. She studied Bilingualism and DysTEFL (Dyslexia and TEFL) at the Universities of Birmingham and Lancaster.

Greci Cristina Queiroz Taylor has 15 years' experience in EAL/EFL, having helped over 300 KS2 EAL pupils to "make rapid progress" (Ofsted Report 2017). She has a degree in Linguistics, a CELTA certificate from Cambridge University, a Diploma in Foreign Language Teaching and a Masters degree in Applied Linguistics and ELT from Nottingham University.

Written by Sally Roberts and Greci Cristina Queiroz Taylor

Editors: Keith Blackhall, Sam Norman, Rosa Roberts, Hayley Shaw.
Reviewed by Juliette Green.
With thanks to Glenn Rogers for the proofreading.

Voice artists for online audio tracks: Eben O'Brien, Phoebe Mullen and Sam Norman.

ISBN: 978 1 78908 799 4

Graphics used throughout the book © www.edu-clips.com
Printed by Zenith Print & Packaging Ltd, Pontypridd.
Based on the classic CGP style created by Richard Parsons.

Text, design, layout and original illustrations © Coordination Group Publications Ltd. (CGP) 2021
All rights reserved.

Photocopying this book is not permitted, even if you have a CLA licence.
Extra copies are available from CGP with next day delivery • 0800 1712 712 • www.cgpbooks.co.uk

How to Use this Book

Working with Children with EAL

- As most of the instructions will be beyond their reading level, children will need to work with an adult or '**Helper**' to use this book.
- The same types of activities are **repeated** though, so in time children should be able to complete many tasks **independently**.
- The activities work really well when children work in **pairs** or **small groups**. Encourage the children to read out their work to you, and to each other.
- Involving children **without EAL** in your teaching is also a great idea — these children will learn a lot about the English language from teaching non-native speakers.

Features of the pages

Every topic of this book is spread over two pages, and follows a similar structure:

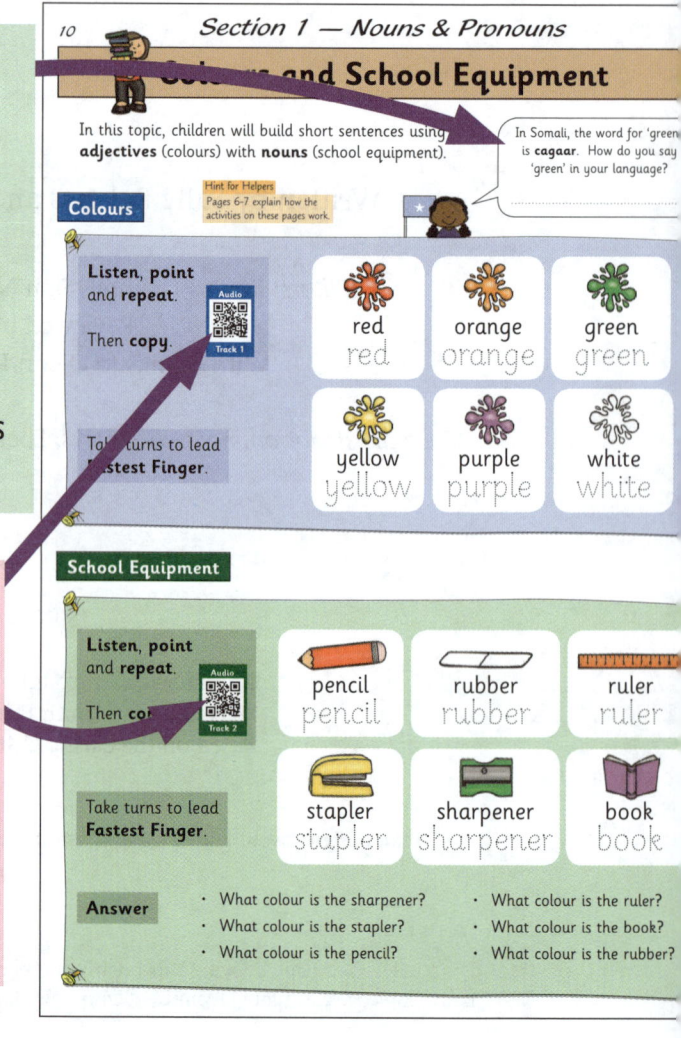

Children are introduced to words and structures in other languages and are invited to think about their **first language**.

- This demonstrates to the child that their first language is **valued**.
- It also promotes **metacognitive thinking** and links learning to ideas already familiar to the children.

The language learning begins with **listening** and **speaking** activities. You can access the audio tracks by scanning the QR code, or by going to:
www.cgpbooks.co.uk/EAL-book-one

You may prefer to deliver these activities without using the recorded audio. There are tips for this on page 6.

How to Use this Book

Phonics

- Accurate phonic decoding skills give children the tools they need to extend their own vocabulary through reading.

- Pages 46-48 have exercises to help children learn the letters and sounds of English.

- It's a good idea to use these pages regularly to help children practise and develop their phonics skills.

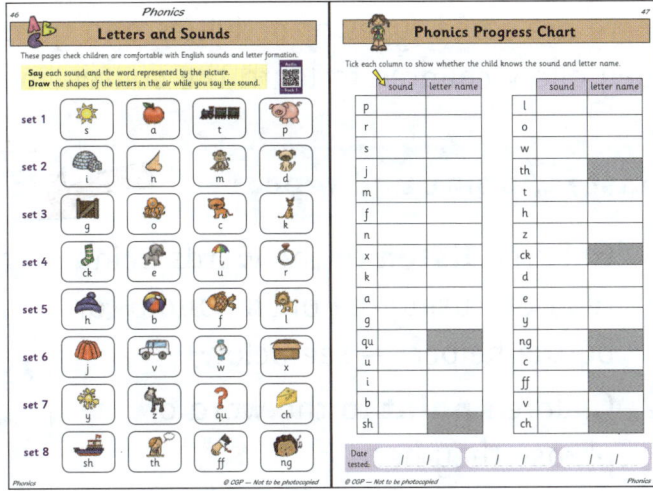

- Some children may appear to read English quite fluently but inaccuracy in pronunciation can make even known words unintelligible — adding to comprehension problems. Particular care is needed with vowel sounds.

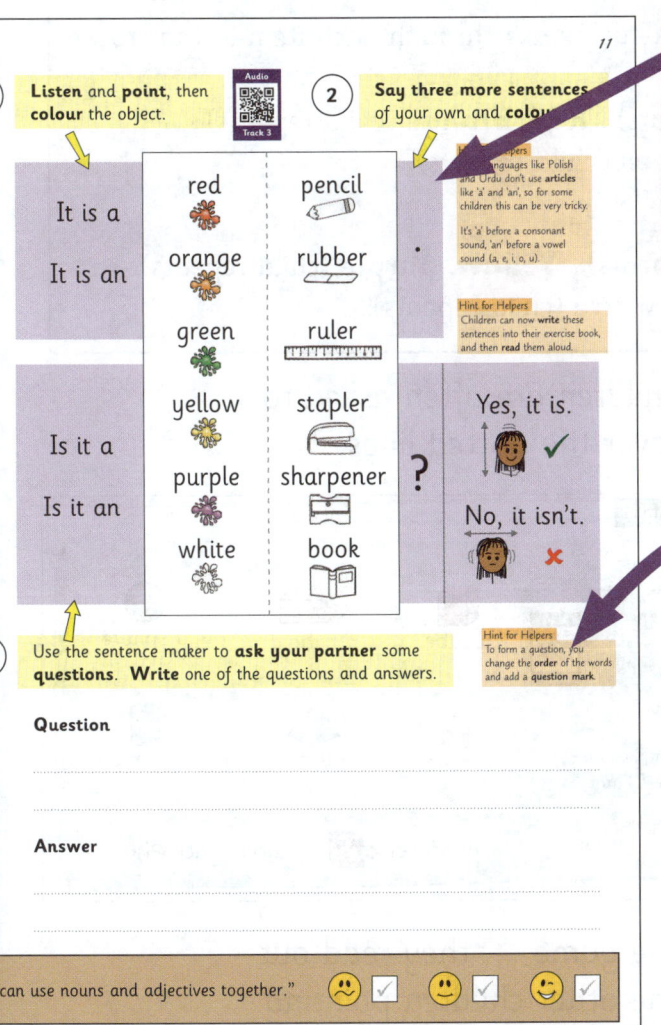

Sentence makers like this are a key feature of this book. They enable children to create their own grammatical sentences independently.

To reinforce their learning, encourage children to copy out sentences into an **exercise book**, and then read them back to you, or to each other.

Hints for Helpers give tips on how you can help children further. They will also point out common **errors** made by children with EAL.

Children with EAL benefit from large amounts of repetition, so it's a good idea not to rush through the activities. Depending on the child's level of English, each topic may take two lessons or more to complete.

How to Use this Book

Activities

There are some types of activities and games which are used throughout this book. They allow children to learn the content of each topic in a fun and engaging way.

Listen, point and repeat

1. Children **listen** to the words being read out using the online audio (or by the helper — see below).
2. Children **point** to the word or phrase they hear.
3. Children **repeat** the words or phrases as they point to them.

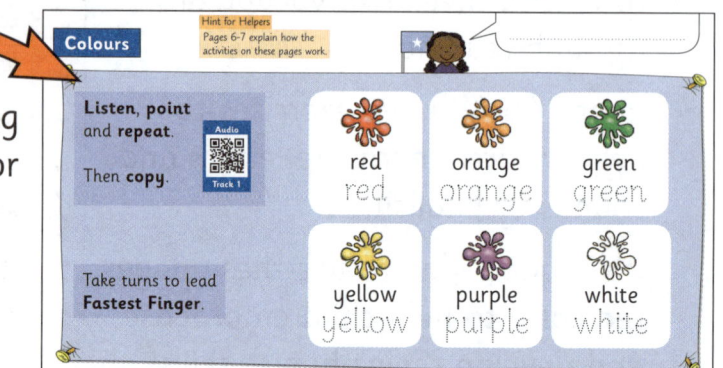

You may prefer to say the words and phrases **yourself** rather than using the online audio. This allows you to adjust the amount of **repetition** and the **pace** according to the level of the child.

It's good to introduce each word or phrase, then cycle back through each item in that row. For example:

'**Red** (child repeats) - **Orange** (child repeats) - **Red, orange** (child repeats) - **Green** (child repeats) - **Red, orange, green** (child repeats)'

Then do the same with the second row:

'**Yellow** (child repeats) - **Purple** (child repeats) - **Yellow, purple** (child repeats) - **White** (child repeats) - **Yellow, purple, white** (child repeats)'

After 'Listen, point and repeat', children are often asked to **copy** the vocabulary by writing over the dotted lines.

Fastest Finger

1. You say one of the words or phrases being taught. Children **point** to what they've heard **as fast as possible**, competing against each other to see who has the Fastest Finger.

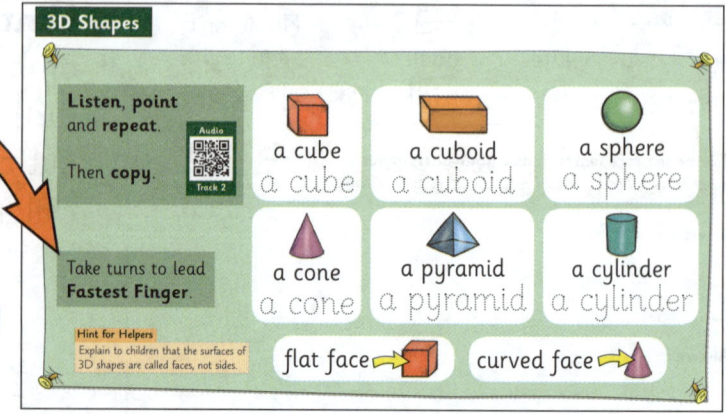

2. Children then take it in turns to **lead** the game — they read out the words and phrases, with you and the other children pointing.

How to Use this Book

Rainbow Underline

1. Children will need a **red**, **blue** and **green pencil** for this activity.
2. Children look at the sentence maker and **listen** to three sentences read out in the audio tracks or by you.
3. Children **underline** the words used in each sentence with the **same coloured pencil**.
4. They underline the first sentence in red, the second in blue and the third in green.
5. Encourage children to read and copy out the sentences afterwards.

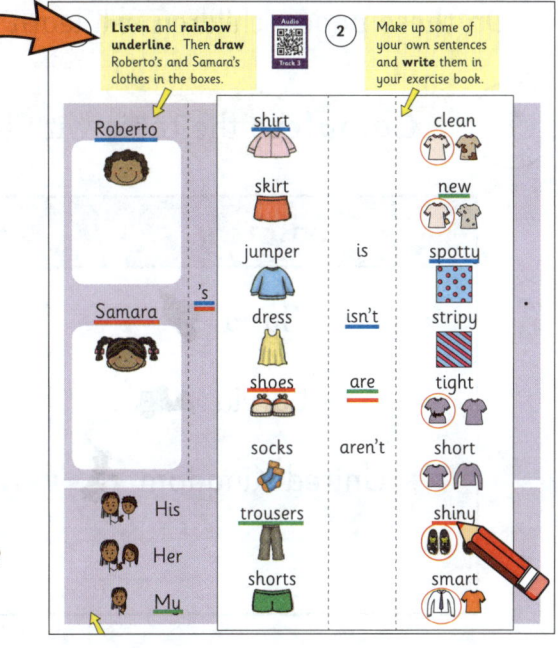

Charades

1. Agree on an **action** to represent each word or phrase.
2. You say the word or phrase and children do the matching action.
3. Then you perform the action and the children call out the word or phrase.
4. Children can play the game in pairs or small groups.

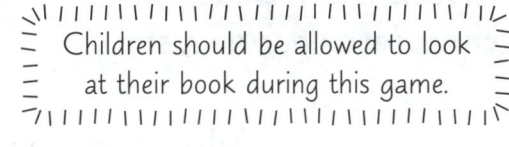

Children should be allowed to look at their book during this game.

Simon Says

1. Children start the game with three lives.
2. You give **commands** that include one of the words being taught.
3. If you start the command with "Simon says...", children should do the action.
4. If you give a command **without** saying "Simon says..." and children do the action, they lose a life.
5. Children can then **lead** a game of Simon Says.

About Me

On these pages, children will learn how to **talk about themselves** and their **hobbies**.

1 **Complete** the table with your **country**, **nationality**, and **first language**.

country	nationality	first language
Syria	Syrian	Arabic
Latvia	Latvian	Latvian
United Kingdom	British	English

2 **Listen** and **repeat**, then **complete** your own story.

Hint for Helpers
Check children can hear the difference between 'Latvia' and 'Latvian' and 'Syria' and 'Syrian'.

My name is Fahad. I am 11 years old.

I am from Syria. I am Syrian.

I speak Arabic.

My name is Gerda. I am 7 years old.

I am from Latvia. I am Latvian.

I speak Latvian and Russian.

My name is .... I am .... years old.

I am from .... I am ....

I speak ....

3 Listen and point, then repeat what Fahad and Gerda say.

I have [short / medium length / long] [black hair / blond hair / brown hair] and [brown eyes. / blue eyes. / green eyes.]

4 Use the sentence maker to write your own description.

I have ....
and ....

5 Listen and point, then repeat what Fahad and Gerda say.
Then play a game of charades using the actions in the sentence maker.

I like [swimming / basketball / roller-skating / going to the park / listening to music / riding my bike / gardening] and [ballet / painting / shopping / maths / football / baking / reading] .

6 Now use the sentence maker to write what you like to do.

I like ....
and ....

Hint for Helpers
Children can use their own hobbies to fill in their story if they want to.

"I can talk about myself."

Section 1 — Nouns & Pronouns

Colours and School Equipment

In this topic, children will build short sentences using **adjectives** (colours) with **nouns** (school equipment).

In Somali, the word for 'green' is **cagaar**. How do you say 'green' in your language?

....

Colours

Hint for Helpers
Pages 6-7 explain how the activities on these pages work.

Listen, **point** and **repeat**.

Then **copy**.

Audio Track 1

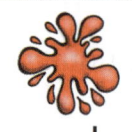 red
 orange
 green

 yellow
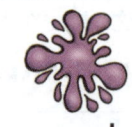 purple
 white

Take turns to lead **Fastest Finger**.

School Equipment

Listen, **point** and **repeat**.

Then **copy**.

Audio Track 2

 pencil
 rubber
 ruler

 stapler
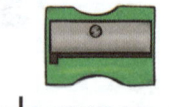 sharpener
 book

Take turns to lead **Fastest Finger**.

Answer
- What colour is the sharpener?
- What colour is the stapler?
- What colour is the pencil?
- What colour is the ruler?
- What colour is the book?
- What colour is the rubber?

11

1 **Listen** and **point**, then **colour** the object.

2 **Say three more sentences** of your own and **colour**.

It is a

It is an

Hint for Helpers
Some languages like Polish and Urdu don't use **articles** like 'a' and 'an', so for some children this can be very tricky.

It's 'a' before a consonant sound, 'an' before a vowel sound (a, e, i, o, u).

Hint for Helpers
Children can now **write** these sentences into their exercise book, and then **read** them aloud.

red	pencil
orange	rubber
green	ruler
yellow	stapler
purple	sharpener
white	book

Is it a

Is it an

?

Yes, it is. ✓

No, it isn't. ✗

3 Use the sentence maker to **ask your partner** some **questions**. **Write** one of the questions and answers.

Hint for Helpers
To form a question, you change the **order** of the words and add a **question mark**.

Question

....

....

Answer

....

....

"I can use nouns and adjectives together."

Numbers and Toys

This topic gets children to make sentences using **numbers** and **singular** and **plural nouns**.

In Romanian, the words for 'one, two, three' are **unu, doi, trei**. How do you say this in your language?

....

Numbers

Listen, point and repeat.

Then **copy**.

Audio Track 4

Take turns to lead **Fastest Finger**.

| 1 one | 2 two | 3 three |
| 4 four | 5 five | 6 six |

Toys

Listen, point and repeat.

Then **copy**.

Audio Track 5

Take turns to lead **Fastest Finger**.

- a ball — a ball
- a doll — a doll
- a hula hoop — a hula hoop
- a dinosaur — a dinosaur
- a skipping rope — a skipping rope

Read the sentences and **colour** the pictures.

- It is a **green** hula hoop.
- It is a **purple** ball.
- It is an **orange** skipping rope.
- It is a **red** dinosaur.
- It is a **yellow** doll.

Section 1 — Nouns & Pronouns © CGP — Not to be photocopied

1 **Listen** and **rainbow underline**.

2 In your exercise book, **Write** the sentences and **draw** a picture for each.

Hint for Helpers
When there is more than one of something, 'is' changes to 'are' and an 's' is usually added to the noun.

There **are** ___ .

two ●●	dinosaur**s**
three ●●●	hula hoop**s**
four ●●●●	skipping rope**s**
five ●●●●●	ball**s**
six ●●●●●●	doll**s**

Are there ___ ?

Yes, there are. ✓

No, there aren't. ✗

3 Use the sentence maker to **ask your partner** some **questions**. **Write** one of the questions and answers.

Hint for Helpers
Aren't is short for are + not.

Question

....
....

Answer

....
....

"I can describe and ask how many things there are."

Section 1 — Nouns & Pronouns

Section 2 — Verbs

Transport

On these pages, children will make sentences using '**There is...**', '**There are...**' and **adjectives**.

In Slovak, the word for 'car' is **auto**. How do you say 'car' in your language?

....

Transport

Listen, point and repeat. Then **copy**. *Audio Track 1*

 a car — a car

 a helicopter — a helicopter

 a bus — a bus

Now take turns to lead Fastest Finger.

 a van — a van

 an ambulance — an ambulance

 a boat — a boat

Adjectives

Hint for Helpers
Remind children that 'a' becomes 'an' before a vowel sound.

Listen, point and repeat. Then **copy**. *Audio Track 2*

 blue — blue

 pink — pink

 black — black

 silver — silver

Now take turns to lead Fastest Finger.

 old — old

 new — new

fast — fast

slow — slow

Listen and repeat.

If there is **one of something**, you say '**There is...**'.

If there is **more than one of something**, you say '**There are...**'.

There is a blue bus.

There are three old car<u>s</u>.

1 **Look** at the pictures. Are the sentences below them correct? **Answer** using a full sentence.

There **is an** old pink car.
No, there is a new pink car.

There **are** two fast ambulances.
....

There **are** five helicopters.
....

There **is** a silver boat.
....

2 **Write** some sentences about these pictures using '**there is**' and '**there are**'.

....
....
....
....

"I know when to use 'there is' and 'there are'."

© CGP — Not to be photocopied

Section 2 — Verbs

Healthy and Unhealthy Food

In this topic, children will use **conjunctions** and **adjectives** to talk about foods they like and don't like.

In Romania, people eat **sarmale** with **mamaliga**. Do you have a favourite food from your country?

Food

Listen, point and **repeat**. Then **copy**. (Audio Track 3)

Now take turns to lead **Fastest Finger**.

| grapes | olives | pizza | chips |
| lettuce | chocolate | burgers | fish |

Can you say any of these foods in another language? Do any sound like the English words?

Adjectives

Listen, point and **repeat**. Then **copy**. (Audio Track 4)

Now, take turns to lead **Fastest Finger**.

| healthy | unhealthy | sweet |
| fresh | savoury | juicy |

With a partner, **decide** which of the foods in the blue box are healthy and which are unhealthy.

In English, **adjectives** come **before** the **noun**.

I like **sweet** **grapes**.

① Use the sentence maker to **make** some positive sentences using 'I like...'. Then **write** one of them below.

....

② **Make** some negative sentences using 'I don't like...'. Then **write** one of them below.

....

③ **Write** a sentence saying two foods you like.

I like sweet grapes **and** fresh chips.

....

④ **Join** a positive and a negative sentence using '**but**'.

I like sweet grapes **but** I don't like healthy fish.

....

"I can use adjectives and conjunctions."

Talking about Pets

This topic gets children to use **verbs** to talk about what pets **can** and **can't** do.

In Bangla, the word for 'dog' is কুকুর (**kukura**). Do you have a pet? Have you ever had a pet?

Pets

Listen, **point** and **repeat**. Then **copy**.
Audio Track 5

 a cat
a cat

 a fish
a fish

 a hamster
a hamster

Now take turns to lead **Fastest Finger**.

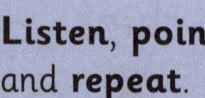 a dog
a dog

 a budgie
a budgie

 a tortoise
a tortoise

With a partner, take it in turns to tell each other what **colour** to make each animal. E.g. 'Colour the dog **brown**.'

Verbs

Listen, **point** and **repeat**. Then **copy**.
Audio Track 6

 run
run

 play
play

 purr
purr

Now take turns to lead a game of **Charades** or **Simon Says**.

 bark
bark

 fly
fly

 swim
swim

Hint for Helpers
See p.7 for instructions on how to play these games.

① **Listen** and **rainbow underline**.

② Make some of your own **sentences** using **'and'** / **'or'**.

A cat **can** run **and** play.

A cat **can't** fly **or** bark.

Hint for Helpers
Join two positive ideas with 'and'.
You join two negative ideas with 'or'.

Hint for Helpers
Point out to children that:
can't = can + not
don't = do + not

A ___ can / can't ___ run / play / purr / bark / fly / swim .

Can a ___ cat / dog / fish / hamster / tortoise / budgie ___ run / play / purr / bark / fly / swim ?

Yes, it can.
No, it can't.
I don't know.

③ **Listen** and **rainbow underline** using three new colours.

④ Use the sentence maker to **ask your partner** some **questions**. Then, **write** the **questions** and **answers** in your exercise book.

"I can make sentences using 'can' and 'can't'." ✓ ✓ ✓

Numbers and Parts of the Body

In this topic, children will use **numbers** to build sentences which include **singular** and **plural nouns**.

In Albanian, the word for 'ten' is **dhjetë**. How do you say 'ten' in your language?

....

Numbers

Listen, point and repeat.

Then **copy**.

Audio Track 9

| 7 seven | 8 eight | 9 nine |
| 10 ten | 11 eleven | 12 twelve |

Parts of the Body

Listen, point and repeat.

Then **copy**.

Audio Track 10

| legs | fingers | ears |
| legs | fingers | ears |

Take turns to lead **Fastest Finger**.

| tails | noses | feet |
| tails | noses | feet |

Listen and **repeat**.

I **have** one nose.

Two dogs **have** two nose**s**.

Hint for Helpers
When it's a single thing in the third person, use 'has' rather than 'have'.

A dog **has** one nose.

Section 2 — Verbs © CGP — Not to be photocopied

1 **Listen** and **rainbow underline**.

2 Use the **sentence maker** to write some more sentences in your exercise book.

I have	no
	1
	2
	3
2 dogs have	4
	5
3 dogs have	6
	7
	8
	9
A dog has	10
	11
	12

leg(s)
finger(s)
ear(s)
tail(s)
nose(s)
feet

Hint for Helpers
The sentence maker uses numerals (e.g. '2') rather than the written words (e.g. 'two') in order to make the activities more manageable for the children.

Hint for Helpers
When asking a question using 'How many...?', the noun is always plural. E.g. 'How many fingers do you have?'

How many		you		
	do	2 dogs		have?
		3 dogs		
	does	a dog		

Hint for Helpers
When it's a single thing in the third person, use 'does' rather than 'do'.

3 **Listen** and **rainbow underline** using three new colours. Then **write** the questions out and **answer** them.

4 In your exercise book, **write** some questions of your own using the sentence maker, then **read** them to your partner so they can **answer** them.

"I can create sentences talking about different parts of the body."

Section 3 — Adjectives & Prepositions
Talking about Feelings

On these pages, children will use **adjectives** to build sentences to describe how they are feeling.

 In Chichewa, the words for 'I'm happy' are **ndili wokondwa**. How do you say this in your language?

....

Feelings

Listen, point and **repeat**. Then **copy**.

 Audio Track 1

Agree an action for each feeling and take turns to play **Charades** then **Simon Says**.

I'm sad
I'm sad

I'm worried
I'm worried

I'm tired
I'm tired

I'm hungry
I'm hungry

I'm happy
I'm happy

I'm angry
I'm angry

Hint for Helpers
Remind children that 'I'm' is short for 'I am'.

More Feelings

 How do you feel about learning English? How do you feel about school?

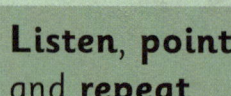

Listen, point and **repeat**. Then **copy**.

 Audio Track 2

Agree an action for each feeling and take turns to play **Charades** then **Simon Says**.

I'm sorry
I'm sorry

I'm confused
I'm confused

I'm ill
I'm ill

I'm surprised
I'm surprised

I'm excited
I'm excited

I'm scared
I'm scared

1 **Play** this game with a partner.

Hint for Helpers
Children will need two different coloured pencils, two counters and a dice to play.

Take it in turns to roll the dice and move your counter. Say the feeling you land on and use your coloured pencil to put a tick next to it in the boxes below. The first to tick all the feelings wins!

◯ I'm sad ◯   ◯ I'm hungry ◯   ◯ I'm happy ◯
◯ I'm tired ◯   ◯ I'm worried ◯   ◯ I'm angry ◯

2 **Listen** to the sentences. **Join** the feelings to a reason, then **read** the sentence pairs to your partner and **copy** them into your exercise book.

Audio Track 3

I'm sorry. ———— I have a headache.

I'm frustrated.   I don't know what to do.

I'm confused.   I don't like the dark.

I'm excited.   I lost my reading book.

I'm scared.   It's my birthday tomorrow.

I'm ill.   I don't know the word in English.

"I can talk about my feelings."

Section 3 — Adjectives & Prepositions

At the Beach

In this topic, children will make sentences using **singular** and **plural nouns** and **prepositions of place**.

Have you been to a beach? Which country was it in?

Beach Objects

Listen, point and repeat. Then copy.

- a net
- a bucket
- sand
- an ice cream
- a crab
- a spade
- shells
- sunglasses

Take turns to lead **Fastest Finger**.

Prepositions

Listen, point and repeat. Then copy.

- in
- on
- under

Take a small cup. **Draw** an ice cream on one piece of paper and some sunglasses on another. Then **demonstrate** and **say** some sentences.

The ice cream **is** under the cup.

The sunglasses **are** in the cup.

Section 3 — Adjectives & Prepositions

1 **Look** at the pictures, then **answer** the questions.

Use this example to help you.

Is the crab on the net?   No, it isn't.

Is the crab in the net?   ....

Is the crab under the net?   ....

Are the shells in the bucket?   No, they aren't.

Are the shells under the bucket?   ....

Are the shells on the bucket?   ....

2 **Draw** a picture like those above. Use the sentence maker below to **write** three questions to go with it. Get your partner to **answer** the questions.

| Is the | spade / ice cream / sand | in / on | the | crab / net / bucket | ? |
| Are the | sunglasses / shells | under | the | sand / shells | ? |

3 Use the sentence maker to **write** and **answer** some more questions in your exercise book.

"I can use 'in', 'on' and 'under'."

Section 3 — Adjectives & Prepositions

26

Section 4 — Maths Language
2D and 3D Shapes

These pages get children to use **adjectives** to describe 2D and 3D shapes.

In Czech, the word for 'circle' is **kruh**. How do you say 'circle' in your language?

....

2D Shapes

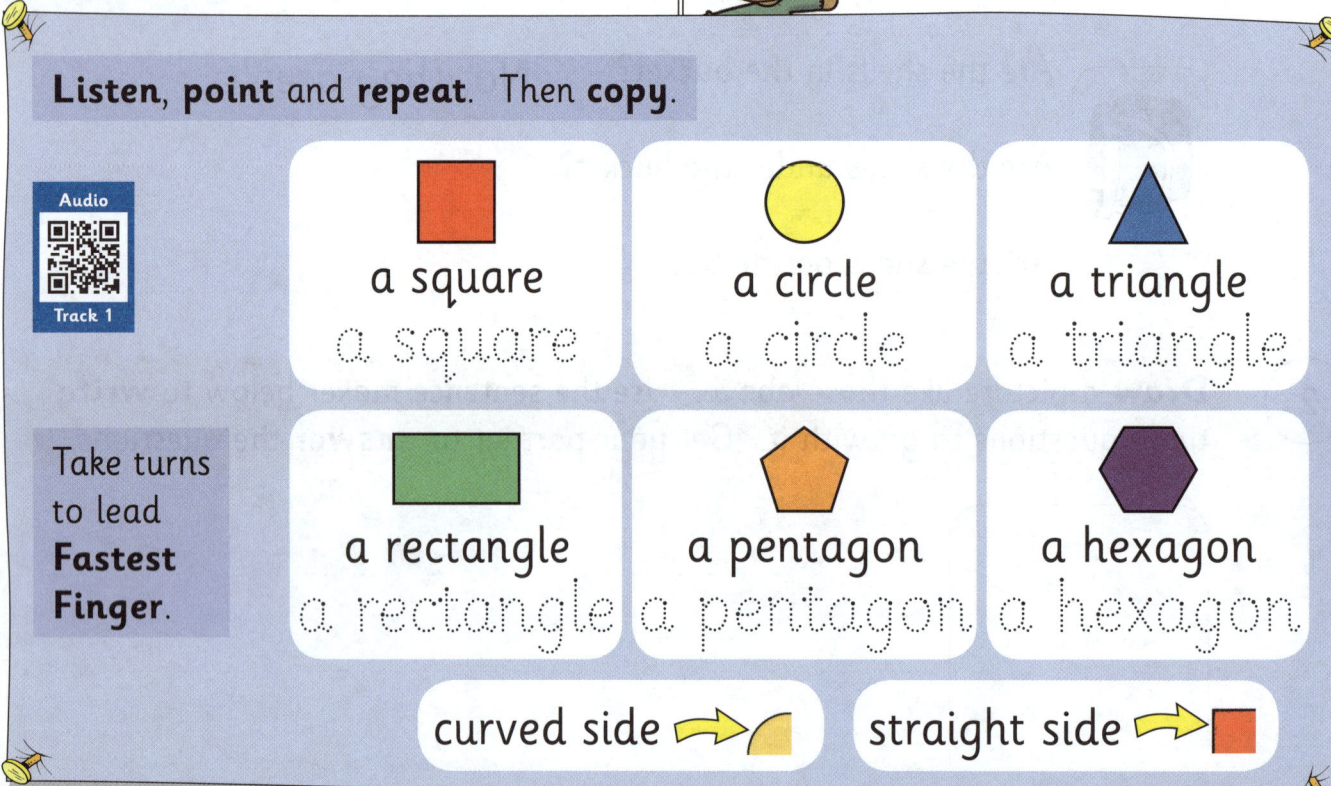

3D Shapes

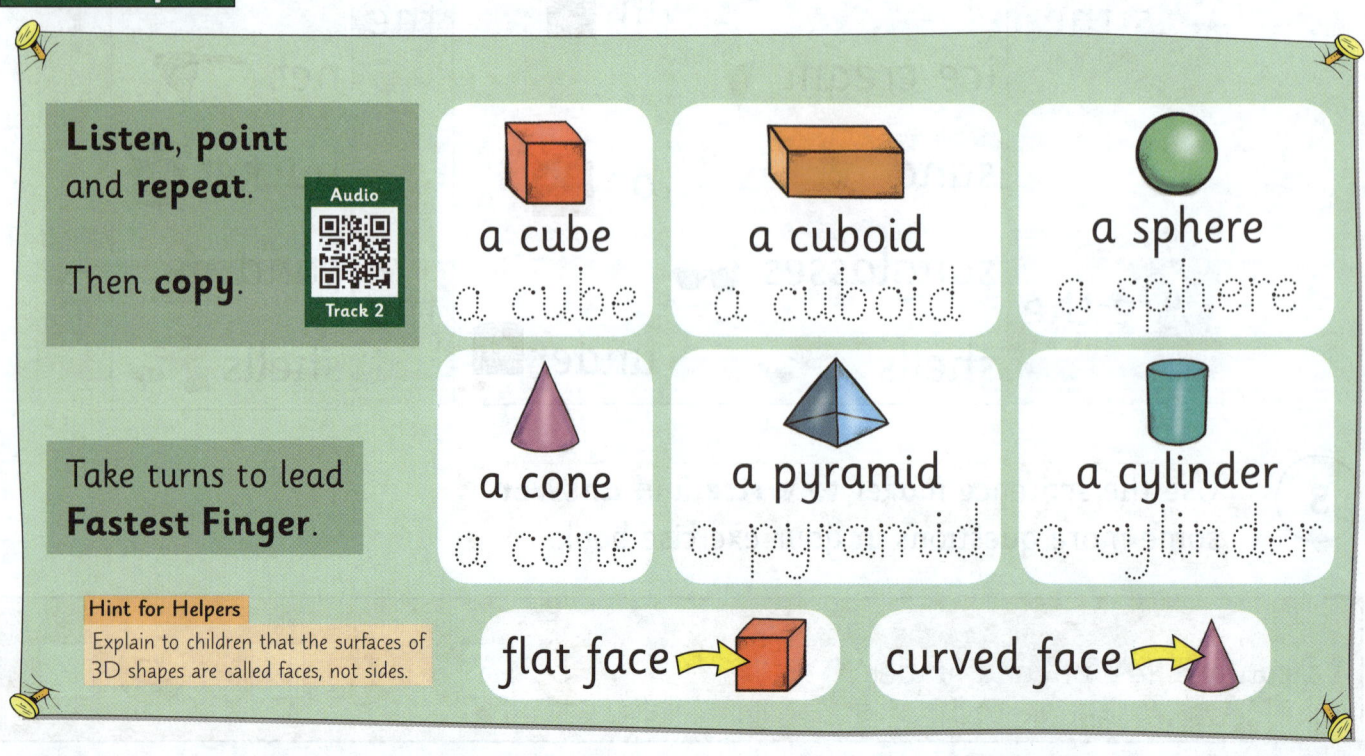

Hint for Helpers
Explain to children that the surfaces of 3D shapes are called faces, not sides.

Section 4 — Maths Language © CGP — Not to be photocopied

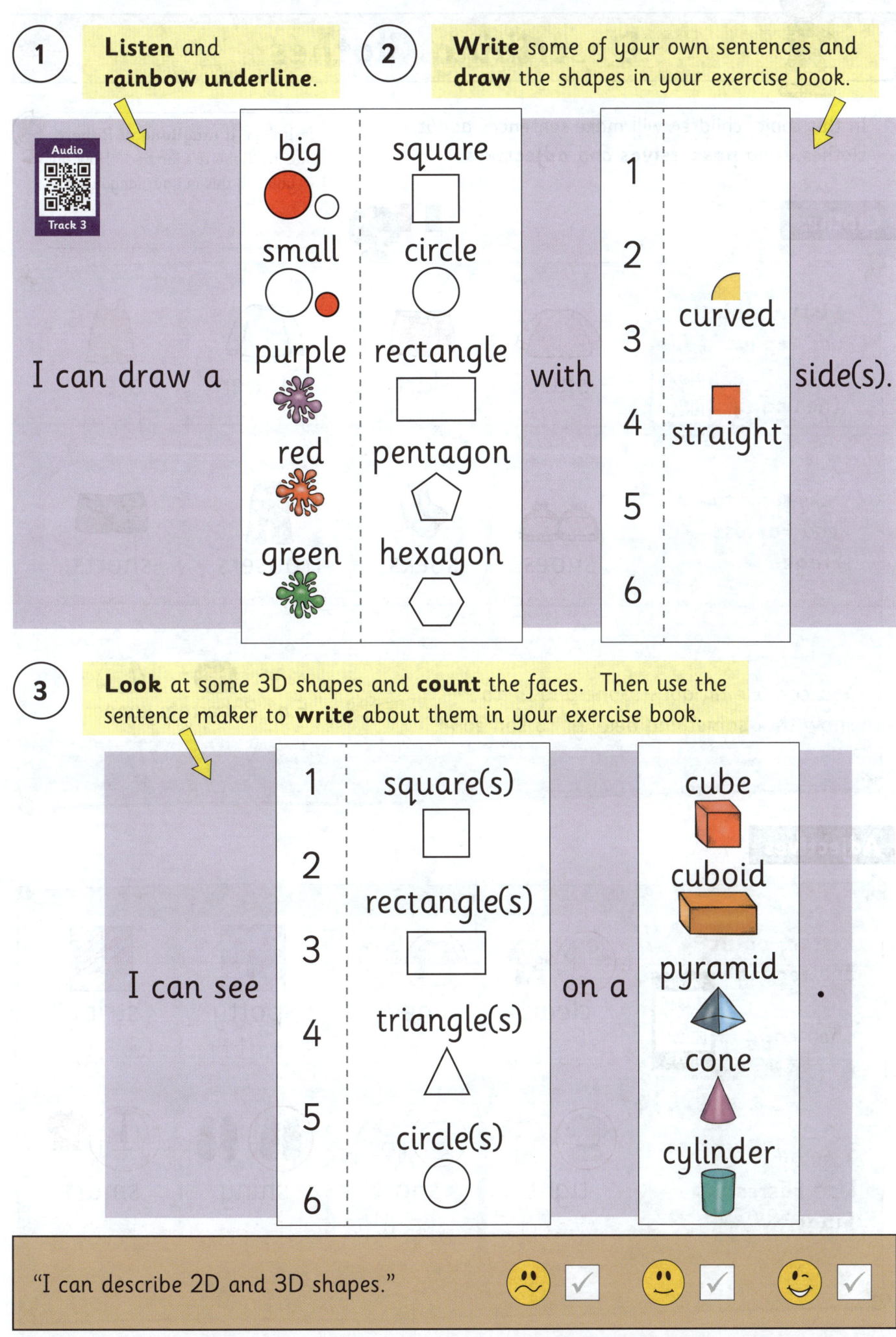

Section 5 — More Nouns & Pronouns

Describing Clothes

In this topic, children will make sentences about clothes using **possessives** and **adjectives**.

In Italian, **il maglione di Roberto** means 'Roberto's jumper'. How do you say this in your language?

....

Clothes

Listen, **point** and **repeat**. Then **copy**. *Audio Track 1*

Take turns to lead **Fastest Finger**.

 shirt — shirt
 skirt — skirt
 jumper — jumper
 dress — dress

 shoes — shoes
 socks — socks
 trousers — trousers
 shorts — shorts

You can use an apostrophe and '**s**' to show that something belongs to someone. → E.g. 'Roberto**'s** jumper'

Adjectives

Listen, **point** and **repeat**. Then **copy**. *Audio Track 2*

Take turns to lead **Fastest Finger**.

 clean — clean
 new — new
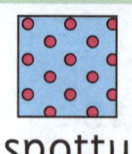 spotty — spotty
 stripy — stripy

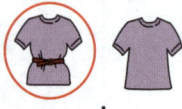 tight — tight
 short — short
 shiny — shiny
 smart — smart

① **Listen** and **rainbow underline**. Then **draw** Roberto's and Samara's clothes in the boxes.

Audio Track 3

② Make up some of your own sentences and **write** them in your exercise book.

Roberto

Samara

's

shirt		clean	
skirt		new	
jumper	is	spotty	
dress	isn't	stripy	
shoes	are	tight	
socks	aren't	short	
trousers		shiny	
shorts		smart	

.

His
Her
My

③ Use the sentence maker to **write** about Roberto or Samara using 'his' or 'her'. Then **write** about your own clothes using 'my'.

"I can show something belongs to someone."

Section 6 — Verbs & Word Order

Days of the Week

This topic gets children to use the days of the week and different **tenses** of 'to be' to construct sentences.

In English, the days of the week have capital letters, but in Spanish they don't, e.g. '**lunes, martes**...' Do the days of the week have capital letters in your language?

Days of the Week

Listen, **point** and **repeat**.

Then **copy**.

Audio Track 1

Monday  Mo

Tuesday  Tu

Wednesday  We

Thursday  Th

Friday  Fr

Saturday  Sa

Sunday  Su

a week

Hint for Helpers
You could show children a calendar to help them learn the days of the week.

Write your favourite day of the week. **Draw** what you do on that day.

Tenses

Listen and **repeat**.

Audio Track 2

You use **is** to talk about the present, **was** to talk about the past and **will be** to talk about the future.

 Today **is** Monday.

 Yesterday **was** Sunday.

Tomorrow **will be** Tuesday.

① **Listen** and **rainbow underline**, then write the sentences and **read** them to your partner.

② Make up some sentences of your own, **read** them out, then **write** them into your exercise book.

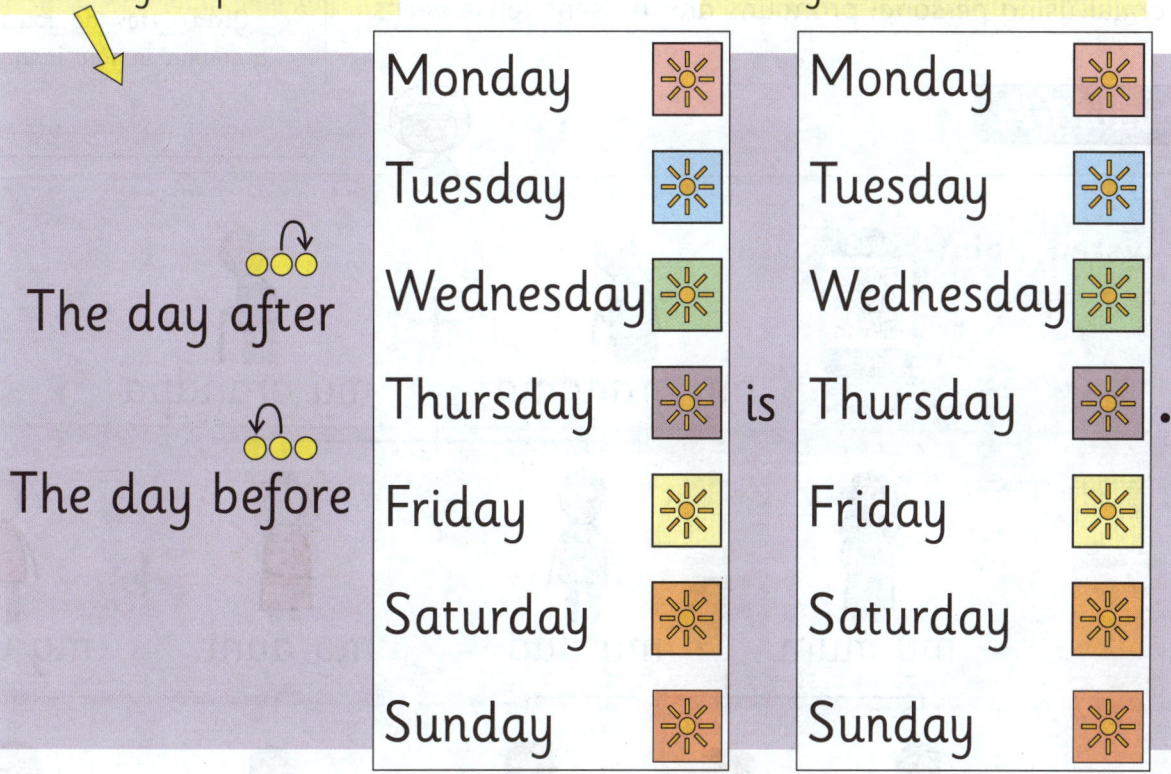

The day after

The day before

③ **Complete** the table with the correct days of the week.

Yesterday **was**	Today **is**	Tomorrow **will be**
	Tuesday	
		Saturday
Tuesday		
	Thursday	

④ What day is it **today**? What day was it **yesterday**? What day will it be **tomorrow**?

....

....

....

"I can use 'yesterday', 'today' and 'tomorrow'."

My Family

In this topic, children will build sentences about their family using personal pronouns and present tense verbs.

In Arabic, 'grandma' is جدة (**jida**). How do you say 'grandma' in your language?

....

Family Tree

Listen, point and repeat.

Audio Track 4

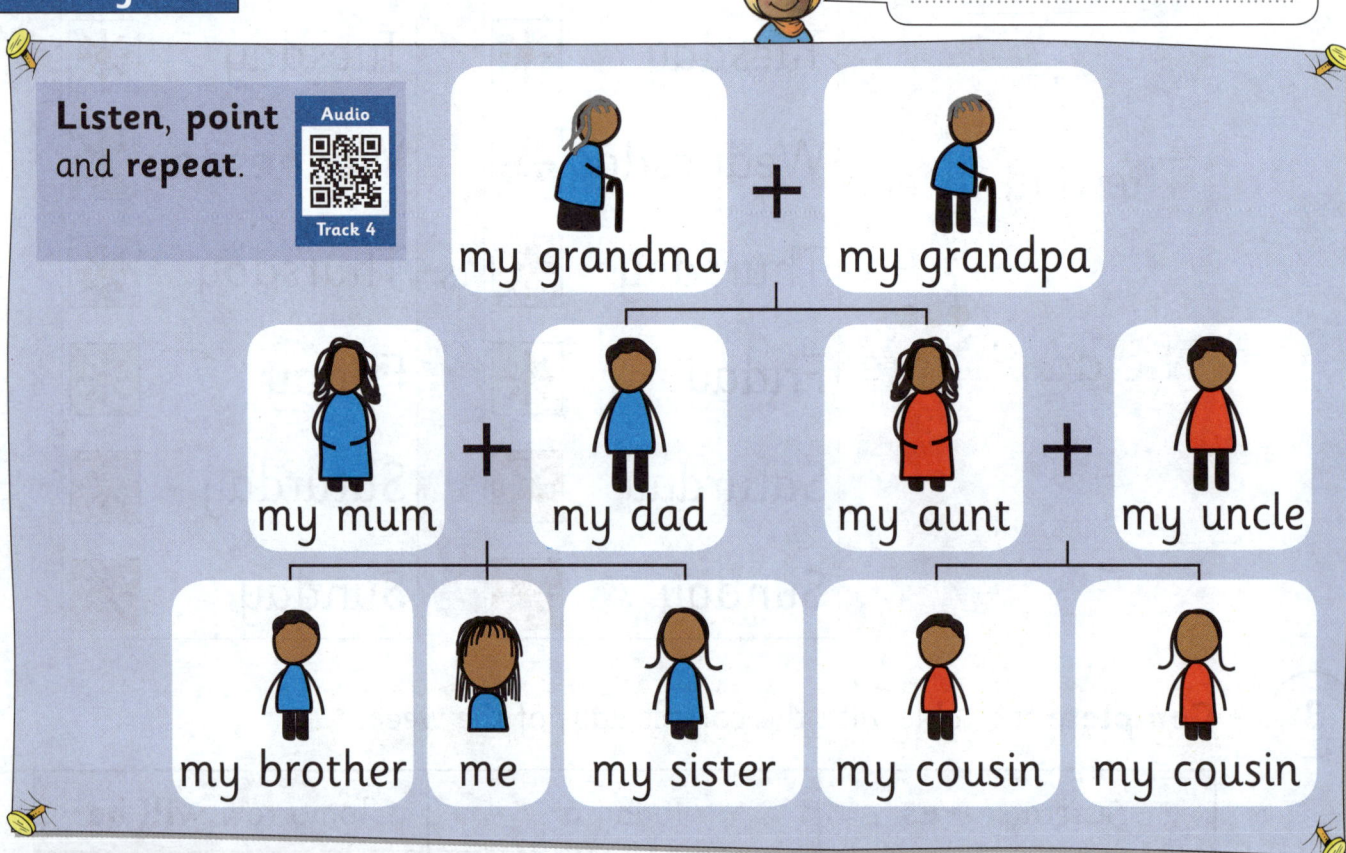

Pronouns

To avoid repeating names all the time, you can use pronouns. These are **I**, **you**, **he**, **she**, **it**, **we**, **you** (plural) and **they**.

When you use **he**, **she** or **it**, you add an **s** to verbs in the present tense.

 I live

you live

we live

you live

 they live

Hint for Helpers
Unlike English, many languages have several words that mean 'you' which are used for different contexts.

 he live**s**

she live**s**

it live**s**

Hint for Helpers
You use 'it' when talking about objects.

Section 6 — Verbs & Word Order
© CGP — Not to be photocopied

1 **Complete** the table with the names of three of your family members and the country they live in.

Family member	Name	Country
brother	Blessing	Nigeria

2 **Use** the completed table to write some sentences using '**s**' and the pronouns **he** or **she** in your exercise book.

Use the example to help you.

My brother'<u>s</u> name is Blessing and he live<u>s</u> in Nigeria.

3 **Listen** and **rainbow underline**.

Audio Track 5

On Mondays,	I walk		to school. 
On Tuesdays,	my dad walk**s**		to the mosque.
On Wednesdays,			
On Thursdays,	my mum eat**s**		an apple. 
On Fridays,	my brothers eat		chocolate cake.
On Saturdays,			
On Sundays,	my uncle read**s**		a recipe. 
At the weekend,	my mum and dad read		emails.

"I can use personal pronouns with verbs correctly."

The Weather

On these pages, children will use **adjectives** and different tenses of '**to be**' to construct sentences.

In Polish, '**jest słonecznie**' means 'it is sunny'. How do you say this in your language?

....

Weather

Listen, **point** and **repeat**. Then **copy**.

Audio Track 6

rainy — rainy
 sunny — sunny
 windy — windy
 snowy — snowy

 warm — warm
cold — cold
 showery — showery
 stormy — stormy

Agree an action for each adjective and play **Charades** or **Simon Says**.

For the present, use **it is**. ➡  It **is** rainy today.

For the past, use **it was**. ➡  It **was** rainy yesterday.

For the future, use **it will be**. ➡ It **will be** rainy tomorrow.

The United Kingdom

There are four countries in the UK. The capital city is London.

Listen, **point** and **repeat**.

Audio Track 7

Take turns to lead **Fastest Finger**.

Hint for Helpers Names of places have capital letters.

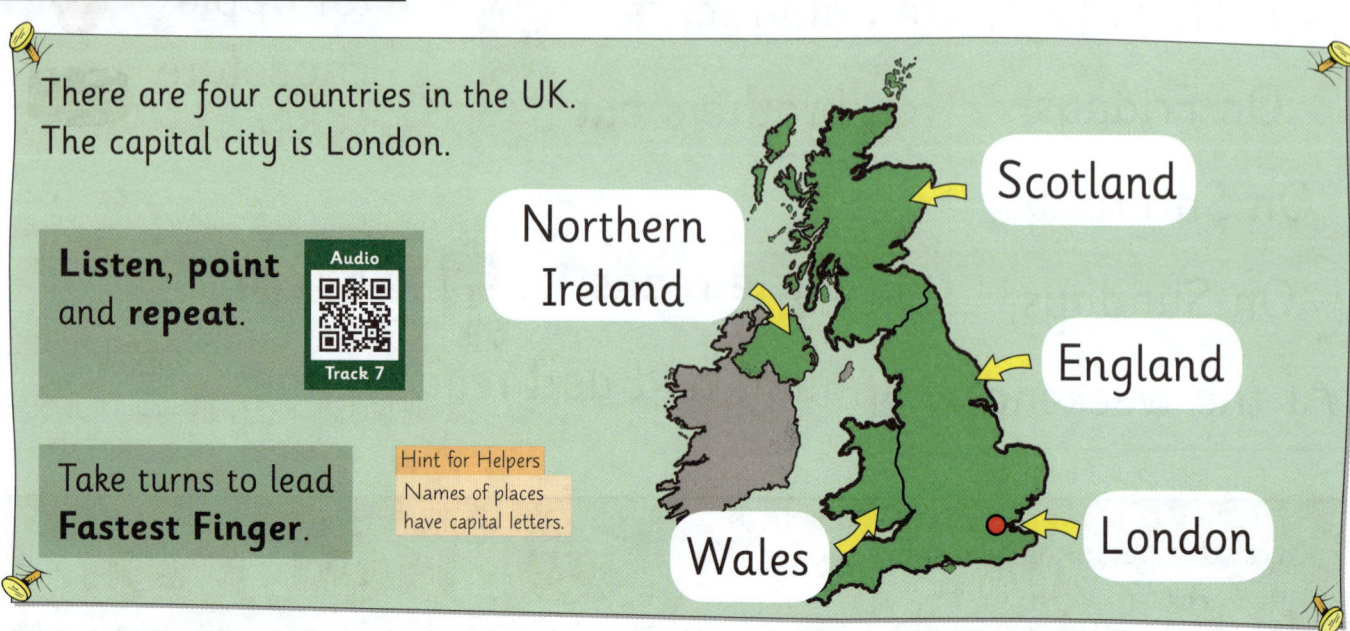

Scotland • Northern Ireland • England • Wales • London

Section 6 — Verbs & Word Order

© CGP — Not to be photocopied

1. **Listen** and **rainbow underline**.

Sentence maker columns:

| It is / It was / It will be | sunny / rainy / windy / snowy / warm / cold / showery / stormy | today / yesterday / tomorrow | in England. / in Scotland. / in Wales. / in Northern Ireland. / in my country. / in London. / in my city. |

2. Use the sentence maker to **make** some sentences of your own, **read** them out, then **write** them in your exercise book.

Hint for Helpers
Encourage children to use the name of the place where they live or used to live.

3. **Draw** a weather map to show your sentences in your exercise book.

"I can use 'it was', 'it is' and 'it will be'."

Wild Animals

In this topic, children will learn how the **subject** comes before the **verb** in English.

In Marathi the word for 'elephant' is हत्ती '**hatti**'. How do you say 'elephant' in your language?

....

Animals

Listen, **point** and **repeat**.

Then **copy**.

Audio Track 9

 elephant
elephant

 monkey
monkey

tiger
tiger

Take turns to lead **Fastest Finger**.

 parrot
parrot

 snake
snake

 spider
spider

Verbs

Listen, **point** and **repeat**.

Then **copy**.

Audio Track 10

 swings
swings

 drinks
drinks

 hunts
hunts

Take turns to lead a game of **Charades** or **Simon Says**.

 flies
flies

 slithers
slithers

 crawls
crawls

The **subject** of a sentence is the person or thing 'doing' the **verb**.

Listen and **repeat**.

subject  verb

The **elephant** **drinks** from the river.

Hint for Helpers
In English, the subject generally comes before the verb, but this is not the case in all languages.

Section 6 — Verbs & Word Order © CGP — Not to be photocopied

1 **Number** the parts of the sentences in the right order.

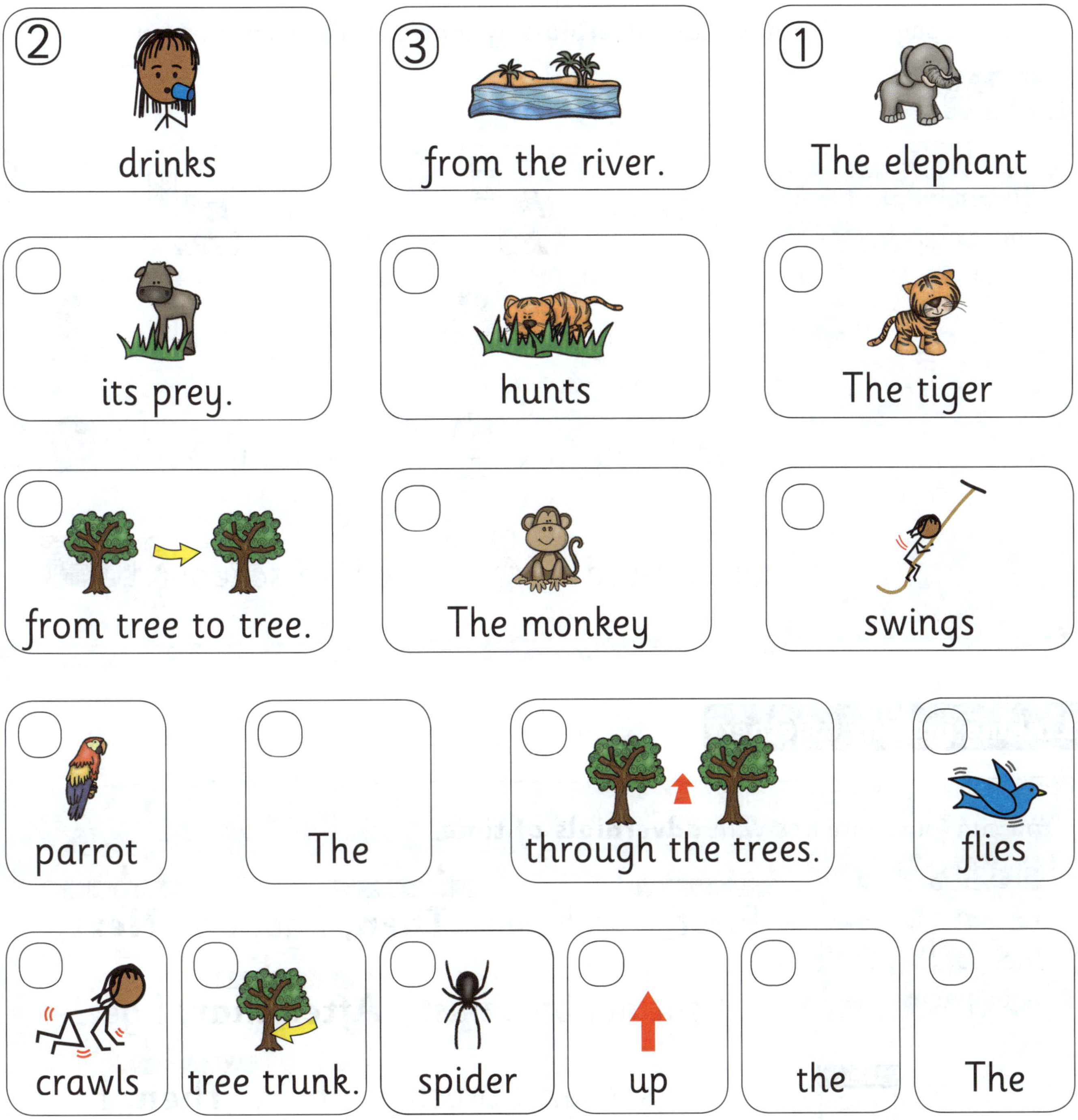

② drinks | ③ from the river. | ① The elephant

○ its prey. | ○ hunts | ○ The tiger

○ from tree to tree. | ○ The monkey | ○ swings

○ parrot | ○ The | ○ through the trees. | ○ flies

○ crawls | ○ tree trunk. | ○ spider | ○ up | ○ the | ○ The

2 **Copy** these sentences into your exercise book and **underline** the subject and verb in each one.

3 **Write** some sentences of your own about animals in your exercise book. Start with a subject and then a verb.

Hint for Helpers
See if children can underline the subject and verb in their own sentences.

"I know that the subject comes before the verb."

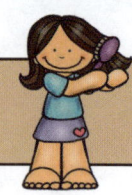

Morning Routine

On these pages, children will use **adverbials of time** to **link** sentences together.

Actions

Listen, **repeat** and **do** each action.

Audio Track 11

- wake up
- get up
- brush my hair
- eat my breakfast
- wash my face
- clean my teeth
- get dressed
- walk to school

Linking actions together

You can join sentences with **adverbials of time**.

Listen and **repeat**. **Follow** the words with your finger.

Audio Track 12

First, I wake up. **Then,** I get up. **Next,** I eat my breakfast. **After that,** I get dressed **and** brush my hair. **Then,** I clean my teeth. **Finally,** I walk to school.

If you start a sentence with **Before**, you swap the order of the actions.

I get dressed. Then I brush my hair.

Before I brush my hair, I get dressed.

© CGP — Not to be photocopied

1 **Number** the activities in the order that you do them.

- ( ) I eat my breakfast
- ( ) I clean my teeth
- ( ) I brush my hair
- ( ) I get dressed
- ( ) I wake up
- ( ) I go to school
- ( ) I wash my face
- ( ) I get up

2 **Use** the adverbials of time to **write** your morning routine below.

Hint for Helpers: When you use '**and**' to join clauses, you **don't** need to repeat 'I'.

First,   Then,   Next,   After that,   Finally,

....

....

....

....

3 Now **write** some sentences about your morning routine that include the word '**before**'.

....

....

....

....

"I can link actions together using adverbials of time."

Things I Like to Do

This topic introduces children to using regular and irregular verbs in the **simple past** tense.

In Portuguese, '**ontem eu comi pizza**' means 'yesterday I ate pizza'. How do you say this in your language?

....

Regular Verbs

When things happened in the past and have finished, you need the **simple past** tense. Usually you add **-ed** to the verb.

Listen, **point**, and **repeat** the verbs and their simple past tense.

Audio Track 13

play	walk	cook	watch
play**ed**	walk**ed**	cook**ed**	watch**ed**

Today I play football. → Yesterday I play**ed** football.

Hint for Helpers
The suffix -ed normally sounds like 'd', but sometimes it sounds like 't', e.g. 'walked'.

Irregular Verbs

Some verbs don't follow the normal pattern — they are called **irregular verbs**.

Listen, **point**, and **repeat** the verbs and their simple past tense.

Audio Track 14

go	eat	run	sit
went	**ate**	**ran**	**sat**

Today, I eat pizza. → Yesterday, I **ate** pizza.

Section 6 — Verbs & Word Order

41

1 Listen and rainbow underline.

2 Use the sentence maker to write some sentences in your exercise book.

Audio Track 15

Yesterday, I

walk**ed**	to school
	to the shops
play**ed**	on my phone
	hide and seek
cook**ed**	dinner
	spaghetti
watch**ed**	a film
	TV
went	to the park
	to town
ate	pizza
	some cake
ran	outside
	in the garden
sat	under the tree
	on the floor

with my

mum.
friends.
grandma.
brother.
sister.
dad.
aunt.
uncle.

3 Use the past tense verbs to write sentences with your own ideas.

"I can use the simple past tense."

© CGP — Not to be photocopied   Section 6 — Verbs & Word Order

Celebrations

These pages teach children to avoid overusing the **past progressive** when talking about things that happened in the past.

> Have you had a celebration recently? What did you do?

Festivals

Listen, point, and repeat. *Audio Track 16*

At Diwali, we ~~were lighting~~ **lit** candles.

During Ramadan, we ~~were eating~~ **ate** dates after sunset.

Yesterday, I ~~was giving~~ **gave** my friends Christmas presents.

More Irregular Verbs

Hint for Helpers
Children learning EAL often use the past progressive when they should use the simple past.

Listen, point, and repeat. *Audio Track 17*

give → **gave**
sing → **sang**
wear → **wore**
make → **made**

Take turns to lead a game of **Charades** or **Simon Says**.

take → **took**
buy → **bought**
see → **saw**

Section 6 — Verbs & Word Order © CGP — Not to be photocopied

1 **Rewrite** the sentences in the simple past tense.

Hint for Helpers
Explain to children that these are events celebrated by different religions.

Last Diwali, we ~~were wearing~~ wore colourful clothes.

....

....

On Sunday, we ~~were buying~~ new lanterns for Buddha Day.

....

....

Last year, at Hanukkah we ~~were singing~~ Maoz Tzur.

....

....

Grandma ~~was cooking~~ a delicious meal for us last Easter.

....

....

2 **Underline** the verbs in the past progressive, then **rewrite** the passage in the simple past tense in your exercise book.

Last Christmas, I was seeing my family in Brazil. It was great fun! We were giving each other presents, my dad was cooking on the barbecue, my mum was making chocolate ice cream and I was playing in the swimming pool with my cousins. We were taking lots of photographs to show to my family in England.

"I know when to use the simple past tense."

At the Playground

On these pages, children will use nouns with **prepositions and adverbs of movement** to build sentences.

In Argentina, we speak Spanish, and in Spanish the word for a 'swing' is **columpio**. How do you say 'swing' in your language?

....

Prepositions and Adverbs

Listen, point and **repeat**.

Then **copy**.

Audio Track 18

 up
up

 down
down

 forwards
forwards

 over
over

 around
around

 backwards
backwards

Playground

Listen, point and **repeat**.

Then **copy**.

Audio Track 19

Take turns to lead **Fastest Finger**.

Listen and **repeat**.

 slide
slide

 roundabout
roundabout

 see-saw
see-saw

 swing
swing

 climbing frame
climbing frame

 field
field

My friend can slide down the slide.

Hint for Helpers
You don't add an 's' to 'can', even when it's in the third person. This is because 'can' is a modal verb, so its spelling never changes.

Section 6 — Verbs & Word Order

1 **Listen** and **rainbow underline**.

Audio Track 20

In the playground, I can

In the playground, my friend can

climb 	up ↑	the field. 
run 	around	the climbing frame. 
swing 	backwards and forwards	on the swing. 
slide 		on the see-saw.
spin 	down ↓	on the roundabout. 
go 	up and down ↑↓	the slide. 

2 **Write** your own sentences starting with 'In the playground, my friend can'.

....

....

....

....

"I can use prepositions and adverbs of movement."

Phonics

Letters and Sounds

These pages check children are comfortable with English sounds and letter formation.

Say each sound and the word represented by the picture.
Draw the shapes of the letters in the air while you say the sound.

Audio Track 1

set 1	 s	 a	 t	 p
set 2	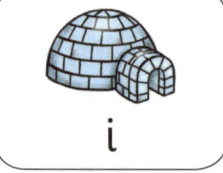 i	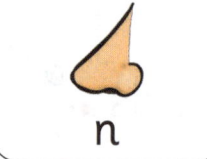 n	 m	 d
set 3	 g	 o	 c	 k
set 4	 ck	 e	 u	 r
set 5	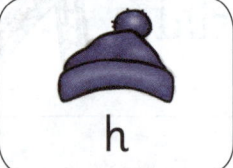 h	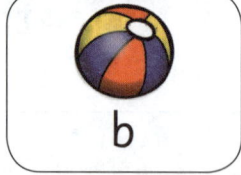 b	 f	 l
set 6	 j	 v	 w	 x
set 7	 y	 z	 qu	 ch
set 8	 sh	 th	 ff	 ng

Phonics Progress Chart

Tick each column to show whether the child knows the sound and letter name.

	sound	letter name		sound	letter name
p			l		
r			o		
s			w		
j			th		▓▓▓
m			t		
f			h		
n			z		
x			ck		▓▓▓
k			d		
a			e		
g			y		
qu		▓▓▓	ng		▓▓▓
u			c		
i			ff		▓▓▓
b			v		
sh		▓▓▓	ch		▓▓▓

Date tested: __ __ / __ __ / __ __   __ __ / __ __ / __ __   __ __ / __ __ / __ __

Short Vowels

This page checks that children can tell the difference between short vowel sounds in English.

Hint for Helpers
Blending sounds means joining the separate sounds in a word together to say the word.

Audio Track 2

a e i o u

1 **Say** the sounds in the words below and blend them. **Read out** the whole word. Then **match** the words to the pictures.

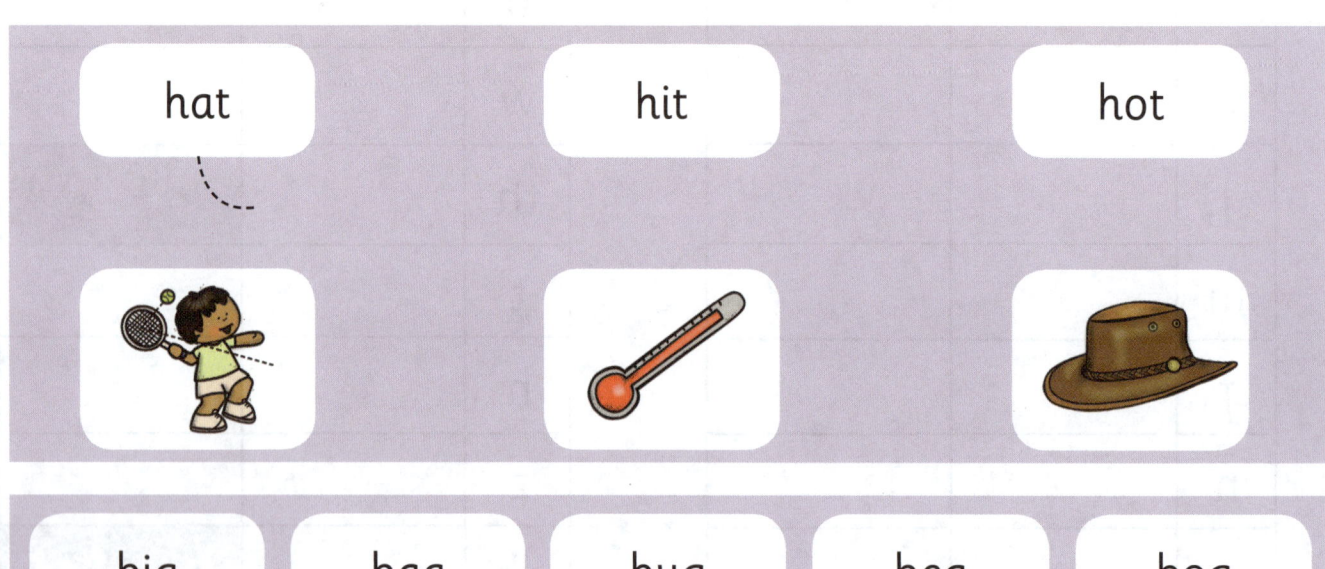

hat   hit   hot

big   bag   bug   beg   bog

  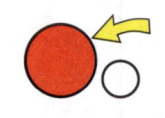  

pot   pit   pat   putt   pet

2 **Point** to each picture and say the sounds individually. E.g., 'p—e—t'.

Phonics © CGP — Not to be photocopied

ALER121